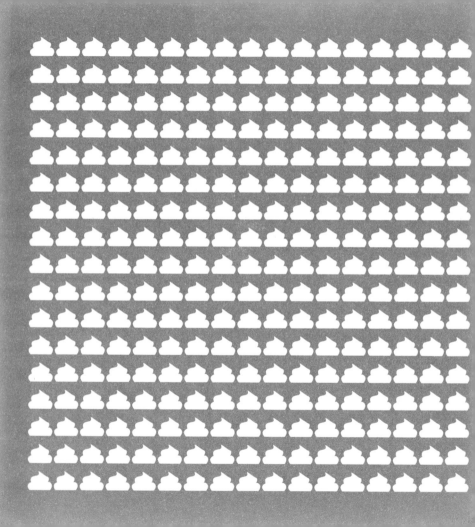

52 THINGS TO LEARN
ON THE LOO

SUMMERSDALE PUBLISHERS LTD
46 WEST STREET
CHICHESTER
WEST SUSSEX
PO19 1RP
UK

WWW.SUMMERSDALE.COM
PRINTED AND BOUND IN MALTA
ISBN: 978-1-84953-784-1

SUBSTANTIAL DISCOUNTS ON BULK QUANTITIES OF SUMMERSDALE BOOKS
ARE AVAILABLE TO CORPORATIONS, PROFESSIONAL ASSOCIATIONS AND OTHER
ORGANISATIONS. FOR DETAILS CONTACT NICKY DOUGLAS BY TELEPHONE:
+44 (0) 1243 756902, FAX: +44 (0) 1243 786300 OR EMAIL: NICKY@SUMMERSDALE.COM

TO ALEXANDER CUMMING
WITHOUT WHOM THIS BOOK
WOULD NOT HAVE BEEN WRITTEN

HUGH JASSBURN HAS SPENT A LOT OF TIME ON THE LOO, AND FROM AN EARLY AGE DECIDED TO MAKE THIS TIME COUNT. FROM EXPANDING HIS KNOWLEDGE OF THE HUMAN BODY TO WONDERING HOW ON EARTH A STARFISH EATS A CLAM, HUGH MADE THE MOST OF THIS QUIET TIME AND LEARNED ABOUT STUFF. STUFF EVERYONE SHOULD KNOW, STUFF YOU WONDER ABOUT, STUFF THAT MAKES YOUR EYEBROWS GO NORTH. USEFUL STUFF, LIKE HOW A FIELD OF PINEAPPLES LOOKS – AND WHEN HIS BRAIN WAS FULL, HE DECIDED TO PUT IT ALL INTO ONE BOOK, JUST FOR YOU. SO SIT BACK, RELAX, AND LEARN...

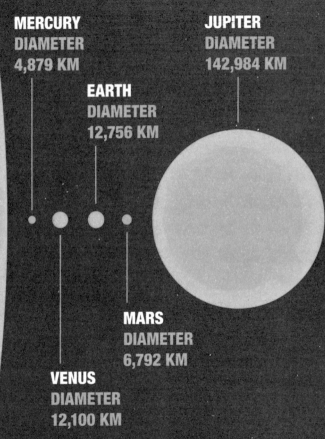

MERCURY
DIAMETER
4,879 KM

JUPITER
DIAMETER
142,984 KM

EARTH
DIAMETER
12,756 KM

SUN
DIAMETER
1,392,000 KM

MARS
DIAMETER
6,792 KM

VENUS
DIAMETER
12,100 KM

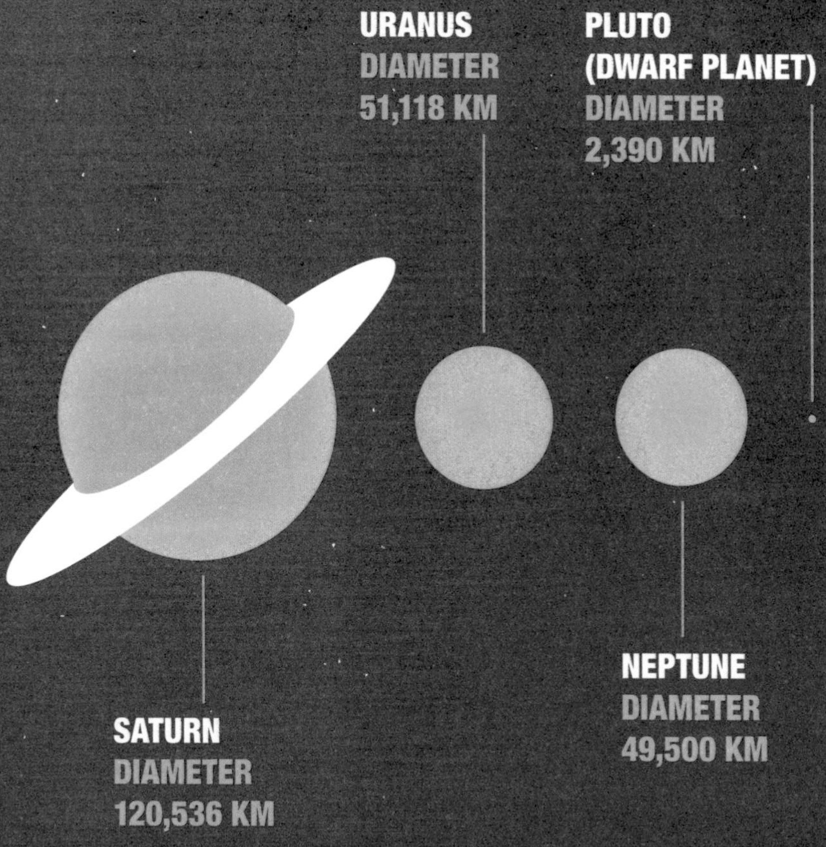

URANUS
DIAMETER
51,118 KM

PLUTO
(DWARF PLANET)
DIAMETER
2,390 KM

SATURN
DIAMETER
120,536 KM

NEPTUNE
DIAMETER
49,500 KM

AFGHANISTAN KABUL **ALBANIA** TIRANA **ALGERIA** ALGIERS **ANDORRA** ANDORRA LA VELLA **ANGOLA** LUANDA **ANTIGUA & BARBUDA** ST JOHN'S **ARGENTINA** BUENOS AIRES **ARMENIA** YEREVAN **AUSTRALIA** CANBERRA **AUSTRIA** VIENNA **AZERBAIJAN** BAKU **BAHAMAS** NASSAU **BAHRAIN** MANAMA **BANGLADESH** DHAKA **BARBADOS** BRIDGETOWN **BELARUS** MINSK **BELGIUM** BRUSSELS **BELIZE** BELMOPAN **BENIN** PORTO-NOVO **BHUTAN** THIMPHU **BOLIVIA** SUCRE **BOSNIA & HERZEGOVINA** SARAJEVO **BOTSWANA** GABORONE **BRAZIL** BRASÍLIA **BRUNEI** BANDAR SERI BEGAWAN **BULGARIA** SOFIA **BURKINA FASO** OUAGADOUGOU **BURMA** NAYPYIDAW **BURUNDI** BUJUMBURA **CAMBODIA** PHNOM PENH **CAMEROON** YAOUNDÉ **CANADA** OTTAWA **CAPE VERDE** PRAIA **CENTRAL AFRICAN REPUBLIC** BANGUI **CHAD** N'DJAMENA **CHILE** SANTIAGO **CHINA** BEIJING **COLOMBIA** BOGOTÁ **COMOROS** MORONI **COSTA RICA** SAN JOSÉ **CROATIA** ZAGREB **CUBA** HAVANA **CYPRUS** NICOSIA **CZECH REPUBLIC** PRAGUE **DEMOCRATIC REPUBLIC OF THE CONGO** KINSHASA **DENMARK** COPENHAGEN **DJIBOUTI** DJIBOUTI **DOMINICA** ROSEAU **DOMINICAN REPUBLIC** SANTO DOMINGO **EAST TIMOR** DILI

ECUADOR QUITO **EGYPT** CAIRO **EL SALVADOR** SAN SALVADOR
ENGLAND LONDON **EQUATORIAL GUINEA** MALABO **ERITREA**
ASMARA **ESTONIA** TALLINN **ETHIOPIA** ADDIS ABABA
FEDERATED STATES OF MICRONESIA PALIKIR **FIJI** SUVA
FINLAND HELSINKI **FRANCE** PARIS **GABON** LIBREVILLE
GAMBIA BANJUL **GEORGIA** TBILISI **GERMANY** BERLIN
GHANA ACCRA **GREECE** ATHENS **GRENADA** ST GEORGE'S
GUATEMALA GUATEMALA CITY **GUINEA** CONAKRY
GUINEA-BISSAU BISSAU **GUYANA** GEORGETOWN **HAITI**
PORT-AU-PRINCE **HONDURAS** TEGUCIGALPA **HUNGARY**
BUDAPEST **ICELAND** REYKJAVIK **INDIA** NEW DELHI **INDONESIA**
JAKARTA **IRAN** TEHRAN **IRAQ** BAGHDAD **IRELAND** DUBLIN
ISRAEL JERUSALEM **ITALY** ROME **IVORY COAST**
YAMOUSSOUKRO **JAMAICA** KINGSTON **JAPAN** TOKYO **JORDAN**
AMMAN **KAZAKHSTAN** ASTANA **KENYA** NAIROBI **KIRIBATI**
TARAWA **KUWAIT** KUWAIT CITY **KYRGYZSTAN** BISHKEK **LAOS**
VIENTIANE **LATVIA** RIGA **LEBANON** BEIRUT **LESOTHO** MASERU
LIBERIA MONROVIA **LIBYA** TRIPOLI **LIECHTENSTEIN** VADUZ
LITHUANIA VILNIUS **LUXEMBOURG** LUXEMBOURG
MACEDONIA SKOPJE **MADAGASCAR** ANTANANARIVO

MALAWI LILONGWE **MALAYSIA** KUALA LUMPUR **MALDIVES** MALÉ **MALI** BAMAKO **MALTA** VALLETTA **MARSHALL ISLANDS** MAJURO **MAURITANIA** NOUAKCHOTT **MAURITIUS** PORT LOUIS **MEXICO** MEXICO CITY **MOLDOVA** CHISINAU **MONACO** MONACO **MONGOLIA** ULAN BATOR **MOROCCO** RABAT **MOZAMBIQUE** MAPUTO **NAMIBIA** WINDHOEK **NAURU** YAREN **NEPAL** KATHMANDU **NETHERLANDS** AMSTERDAM **NEW ZEALAND** WELLINGTON **NICARAGUA** MANAGUA **NIGER** NIAMEY **NIGERIA** ABUJA **NORTH KOREA** PYONGYANG **NORWAY** OSLO **OMAN** MUSCAT **PAKISTAN** ISLAMABAD **PALAU** NGERULMUD **PANAMA** PANAMA CITY **PAPUA NEW GUINEA** PORT MORESBY **PARAGUAY** ASUNCIÓN **PERU** LIMA **PHILIPPINES** MANILA **POLAND** WARSAW **PORTUGAL** LISBON **QATAR** DOHA **REPUBLIC OF THE CONGO** BRAZZAVILLE **ROMANIA** BUCHAREST **RUSSIA** MOSCOW **RWANDA** KIGALI **SAINT KITTS & NEVIS** BASSETERRE **SAINT LUCIA** CASTRIES **SAINT VINCENT & THE GRENADINES** KINGSTOWN **SAMOA** APIA **SAN MARINO** SAN MARINO **SÃO TOMÉ & PRÍNCIPE** SÃO TOMÉ **SAUDI ARABIA** RIYADH **SCOTLAND** EDINBURGH **SENEGAL** DAKAR **SERBIA & MONTENEGRO** BELGRADE

SEYCHELLES VICTORIA **SIERRA LEONE** FREETOWN
SINGAPORE SINGAPORE **SLOVAKIA** BRATISLAVA **SLOVENIA**
LJUBLJANA **SOLOMON ISLANDS** HONIARA **SOMALIA**
MOGADISHU **SOUTH AFRICA** PRETORIA **SOUTH KOREA** SEOUL
SPAIN MADRID **SRI LANKA** COLOMBO **SUDAN** KHARTOUM
SURINAME PARAMARIBO **SWAZILAND** MBABANE **SWEDEN**
STOCKHOLM **SWITZERLAND** BERN **SYRIA** DAMASCUS
TAIWAN TAIPEI **TAJIKISTAN** DUSHANBE **TANZANIA** DODOMA
THAILAND BANGKOK **TOGO** LOMÉ **TONGA** NUKU'ALOFA
TRINIDAD & TOBAGO PORT OF SPAIN **TUNISIA** TUNIS **TURKEY**
ANKARA **TURKMENISTAN** ASHGABAT **TUVALU** FUNAFUTI
UGANDA KAMPALA **UKRAINE** KIEV **UNITED ARAB EMIRATES**
ABU DHABI **UNITED STATES** WASHINGTON DC **URUGUAY**
MONTEVIDEO **UZBEKISTAN** TASHKENT **VANUATU** PORT VILA
VATICAN CITY VATICAN CITY **VENEZUELA** CARACAS
VIETNAM HANOI **WALES** CARDIFF **YEMEN** SANA'A **ZAMBIA**
LUSAKA **ZIMBABWE** HARARE

ELECTRIC TELEGRAPH
1837
SAMUEL MORSE

MORSE SENT HIS FIRST TELEGRAPH MESSAGE IN MORRISTOWN, NEW JERSEY, ACROSS 2 MILES OF WIRE IN 1838. IN 1866 A TELEGRAPH CABLE WAS LAID ACROSS THE ATLANTIC OCEAN FROM THE US TO EUROPE.

FAX MACHINE
1843
ALEXANDER BAIN

**ORIGINALLY PATENTED BY BAIN AS
'THE ELECTRIC PRINTING TELEGRAPH'.
IN 1964 XEROX CORPORATION
PATENTED AND INTRODUCED THE FIRST
COMMERCIALISED MODERN FAX MACHINE.**

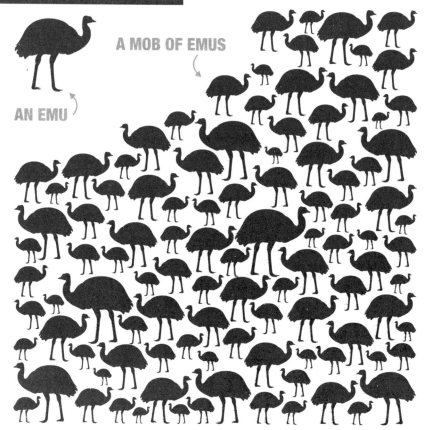

A MOB OF EMUS

AN EMU

A MURDER OF CROWS

A CROW

ROMAN SEWERS
800–735 BC
THE ROMANS!

RICH PEOPLE HAD THEIR OWN TOILETS; THE POOR USED PUBLIC LAVATORIES. THERE WAS NO PRIVACY, JUST STONE SEATS NEXT TO EACH OTHER WITH HOLES AND WATER RUNNING UNDERNEATH.

FLUSHING TOILET
1775
ALEXANDER CUMMING

THE S-SHAPED PLUMBING DESIGN, MODIFIED TO BE A U-SHAPED PIPE IN TODAY'S TOILETS, WAS CREATED TO PREVENT SEWER GASES FROM ENTERING BUILDINGS.

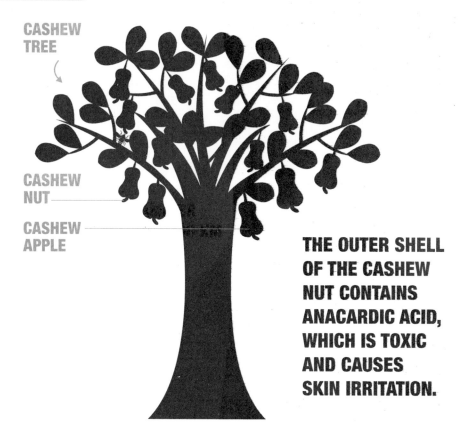

CASHEW
TREE

CASHEW
NUT

CASHEW
APPLE

THE OUTER SHELL OF THE CASHEW NUT CONTAINS ANACARDIC ACID, WHICH IS TOXIC AND CAUSES SKIN IRRITATION.

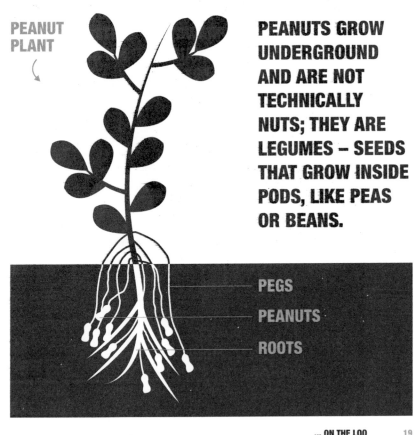

PEANUT PLANT

PEANUTS GROW UNDERGROUND AND ARE NOT TECHNICALLY NUTS; THEY ARE LEGUMES – SEEDS THAT GROW INSIDE PODS, LIKE PEAS OR BEANS.

PEGS

PEANUTS

ROOTS

**FOLD
CORNERS
IN TO MEET
AT CENTRE**

**DROP
FOLDED
PAPER
DOWN IN
FRONT
OF ROLL**

**FOLD IN
EDGES**

**FOLD UP
TO FORM A
TRIANGLE**

PULL DOWN SO TRIANGLE IS MORE CENTRED

FOLD UP BOTTOM EDGE OF TRIANGLE

FOLD CORNERS BEHIND

DONE!

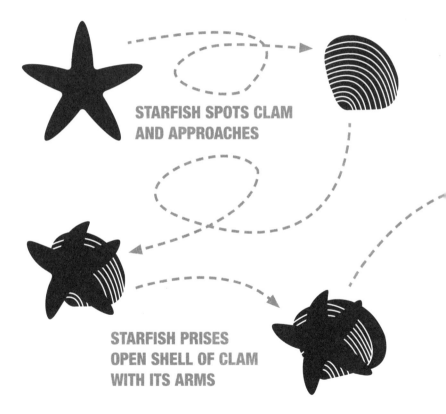

STARFISH SPOTS CLAM
AND APPROACHES

STARFISH PRISES
OPEN SHELL OF CLAM
WITH ITS ARMS

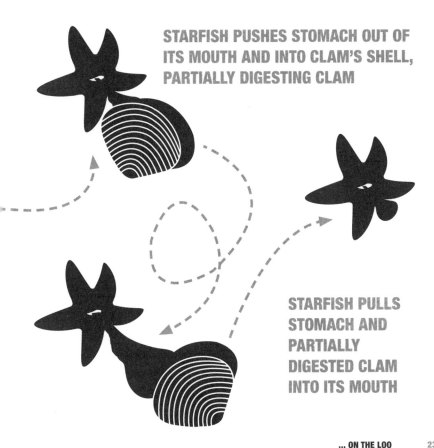

STARFISH PUSHES STOMACH OUT OF ITS MOUTH AND INTO CLAM'S SHELL, PARTIALLY DIGESTING CLAM

STARFISH PULLS STOMACH AND PARTIALLY DIGESTED CLAM INTO ITS MOUTH

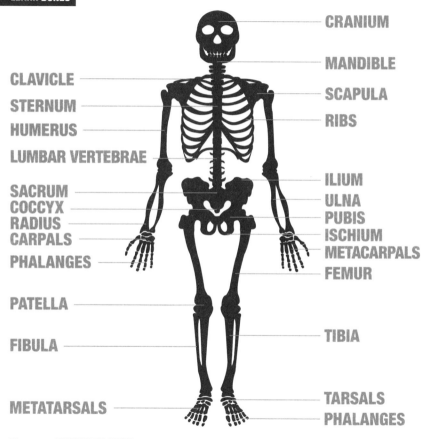

CRANIUM

MANDIBLE

CLAVICLE

SCAPULA

STERNUM

RIBS

HUMERUS

LUMBAR VERTEBRAE

ILIUM

SACRUM

ULNA

COCCYX

PUBIS

RADIUS

ISCHIUM

CARPALS

METACARPALS

PHALANGES

FEMUR

PATELLA

FIBULA

TIBIA

METATARSALS

TARSALS

PHALANGES

THE HUMAN SKELETON HAS OVER 300
BONES AT BIRTH. BONES FUSE TOGETHER
DURING MATURITY LEAVING AN ADULT
HUMAN SKELETON WITH 206 BONES.

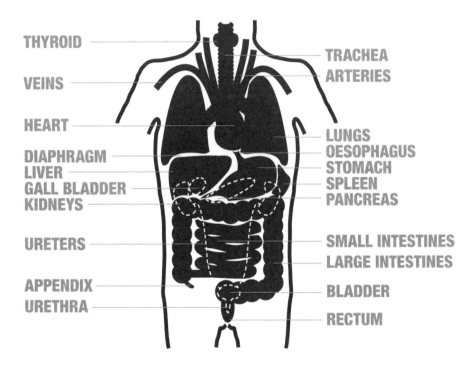

THYROID

VEINS

HEART

DIAPHRAGM
LIVER
GALL BLADDER
KIDNEYS

URETERS

APPENDIX
URETHRA

TRACHEA
ARTERIES

LUNGS
OESOPHAGUS
STOMACH
SPLEEN
PANCREAS

SMALL INTESTINES
LARGE INTESTINES

BLADDER

RECTUM

OUR LARGEST ORGAN IS OUR SKIN, WEIGHING AROUND 3.5 KG AND COVERING OVER 2 SQUARE METERS, COMPARED TO THE HUMAN HEART WHICH WEIGHS AN AVERAGE OF 0.2 KG.

POP-UP TOASTER
1919
CHARLES STRITE

**USING A VERSION OF STRITE'S TOASTER, THE
WATERS-GENTER COMPANY INTRODUCED
THE MODEL 1-A-1 TOASTMASTER IN 1925.
BEFORE ELECTRIC TOASTERS BREAD WAS
TOASTED BY HOLDING A LONG-HANDLED
FORK OVER A FIRE OR KITCHEN GRILL.**

MICROWAVE OVEN
1946
DR PERCY SPENCER

WHILE WORKING ON RADAR SETS, SPENCER NOTICED THE SWEETS IN HIS POCKET MELTING IN FRONT OF AN ACTIVE RADAR. AFTER HEATING OTHER FOODS IN THIS WAY AND DEVELOPING A BOX TO SURROUND THEM, THE MICROWAVE OVEN WAS BORN.

ALBANIA
CKEMI

ANDORRA
HOLA

ARMENIA
BAREV

AUSTRIA
HALLO

AZERBAIJAN
SALAM

BELARUS
VITAYU

BELGIUM
DAG

BOSNIA & HERZEGOVINA
ZDRAVO

BULGARIA
ZDRAVEYTE

CROATIA
ZDRAVO

CYPRUS
GH'YA

CZECH REPUBLIC
AHOJ

DENMARK
HEJ

ESTONIA
TERE

FINLAND
TERVE

FRANCE
BONJOUR

GEORGIA
GAMARJOBA

GERMANY
GUTEN TAG

GREECE
YASSOU

HUNGARY
SZIA

ICELAND
HALLÓ

IRELAND
DIA DHUIT

ITALY
CIAO

KOSOVO
TUNG

LATVIA
SVEIKI

LIECHTENSTEIN
GUTEN TAG

LITHUANIA
LABAS

LUXEMBOURG
MOIEN

MACEDONIA
ZDRAVO

MALTA
HAWN

MOLDOVA
SALUT

MONACO
BONJOUR

MONTENEGRO
ZDRAVO

THE NETHERLANDS
HALLO

NORWAY
HEI

POLAND
CZEŚĆ

PORTUGAL
OLÁ

ROMANIA
BUNĂ

RUSSIA
ZDRAVSTVUJ

SAN MARINO
BUONGIORNO

SCOTLAND
HALÒ

SERBIA
ZDRAVO

SLOVAKIA
AHOJ

SLOVENIA
ŽIVJO

SPAIN
HOLA

SWEDEN
HEJ

SWITZERLAND
GRUETZI

TURKEY
MERHABA

UKRAINE
VITAYU

WALES
SHWMAE

FOLD ONE AND A HALF SQUARES DIAGONALLY

FOLD DIAGONALLY AGAIN

FOLD SO THAT PAPER POINTS UPWARD

LIFT PAPER UP ABOVE ROLL WITHOUT OPENING FOLDS

FOLD CORNERS DOWN

LOWER PAPER ON TO ROLL

DONE!

4.6 BILLION YEARS AGO

EARTH FORMED

1.1 BILLION YEARS AGO

FIRST SEXUALLY REPRODUCING ORGANISMS

530 MILLION YEARS AGO

FIRST FISH

3.8 BILLION YEARS AGO

FIRST LIFE – SINGLE-CELLED ORGANISMS

570 MILLION YEARS AGO

FIRST ARTHROPODS

**385 MILLION
YEARS AGO**

FIRST FORESTS

**320 MILLION
YEARS AGO**

EARLIEST
REPTILES

**475 MILLION
YEARS AGO**

FIRST LAND
PLANTS

**370 MILLION
YEARS AGO**

FIRST
AMPHIBIANS

**225 MILLION
YEARS AGO**

FIRST
DINOSAURS

200 MILLION YEARS AGO

FIRST MAMMALS

130 MILLION YEARS AGO

FIRST FLOWERING PLANTS

65 MILLION YEARS AGO

DINOSAURS BECOME EXTINCT

150 MILLION YEARS AGO

FIRST BIRDS

100 MILLION YEARS AGO

FIRST BEES

2.5 MILLION YEARS AGO
GENUS HOMO EVOLVES

10,000 YEARS AGO
END OF THE LAST ICE AGE

14 MILLION YEARS AGO
FIRST GREAT APES

200,000 YEARS AGO
OUR SPECIES, HOMO SAPIENS, EVOLVES

CAR
1886
KARL FRIEDRICH BENZ

FIRST MODERN AUTOMOBILE POWERED BY AN INTERNAL COMBUSTION ENGINE.

AEROPLANE
1903
THE WRIGHT BROTHERS

**FIRST POWERED FLIGHT LASTED 12 SECONDS
AND TRAVELLED A DISTANCE OF 36.5 METRES.**

A TITTLE

TYPEWRITER

THERE ARE ABOUT 4,500 SPECIES OF MAMMALS. ONLY TWO LAY EGGS: THE DUCK-BILLED PLATYPUS AND THE ECHIDNA.

**APART FROM HUMANS, ELEPHANTS ARE THE
ONLY OTHER MAMMALS WITH A CHIN.**

**NEW
MOON**

**WAXING
CRESCENT**

**FIRST
QUARTER**

**WAXING
GIBBOUS**

DAY 1

DAY 2–6

DAY 7

DAY 8–13

**FULL
MOON**

DAY 14

**WANING
GIBBOUS**

DAY 15–24

**LAST
QUARTER**

DAY 22

**WANING
CRESCENT**

DAY 23–28

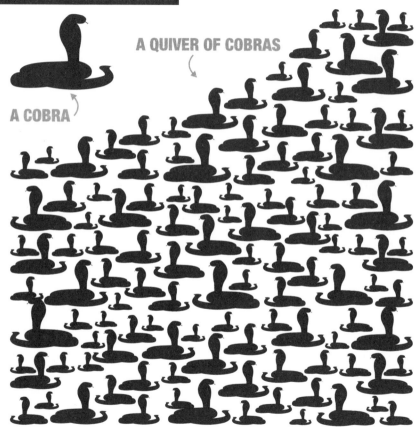

A QUIVER OF COBRAS

A COBRA

A CONGREGATION OF ALLIGATORS

AN ALLIGATOR

0   +1   **+2**   +3   **+4**   +5   **+6**   +7   **+8**   +9   **+10**   +1

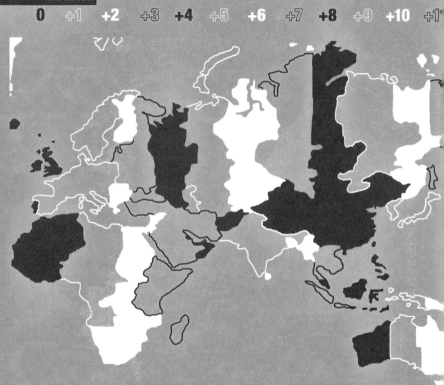

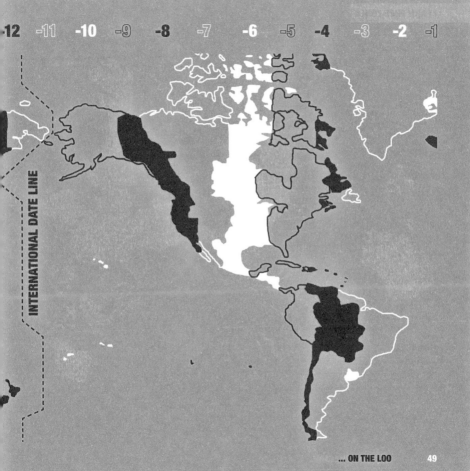

-12 -11 -10 -9 -8 -7 -6 -5 -4 -3 -2 -1

INTERNATIONAL DATE LINE

ALDER   ASH   BEECH   BIRCH

ROWAN   HAWTHORN   HAZEL   HORSE CHESTNUT

ELDER

ELM

OAK

PINE

MAPLE

SYCAMORE

WILLOW

YEW

TOOTHBRUSH
1780
WILLIAM ADDIS

BEFORE THE TOOTHBRUSH, TEETH WERE CLEANED USING A RAG WITH SOOT AND SALT.

ELECTRIC TOOTHBRUSH
1954
DR PHILIPPE-GUY WOOG

ORIGINALLY CREATED FOR PEOPLE WITH LIMITED MOTOR SKILLS AND PHYSICAL DISABILITIES.

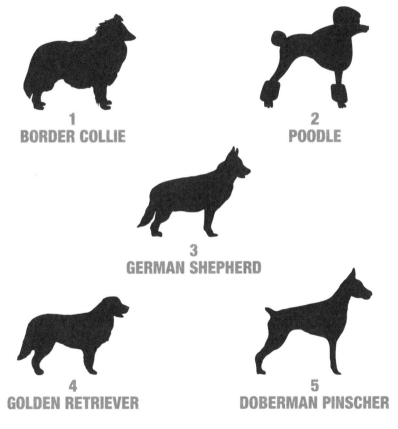

1
BORDER COLLIE

2
POODLE

3
GERMAN SHEPHERD

4
GOLDEN RETRIEVER

5
DOBERMAN PINSCHER

6
SHETLAND SHEEPDOG

7
LABRADOR RETRIEVER

8
PAPILLON

9
ROTTWEILER

10
AUSTRALIAN CATTLE DOG

A FLANGE OF BABOONS

A BABOON

A SLEUTH OF BEARS

A BEAR

ZIP FASTENER
1891
WHITCOMB JUDSON

USED ALMOST EXCLUSIVELY FOR BOOTS AND TOBACCO POUCHES FOR THE FIRST 20 YEARS.

VELCRO
1948
GEORGE DE MESTRAL

THE WORD VELCRO IS A COMBINATION OF TWO FRENCH WORDS: *VELOURS*, MEANING VELVET, AND *CROCHET*, MEANING HOOK.

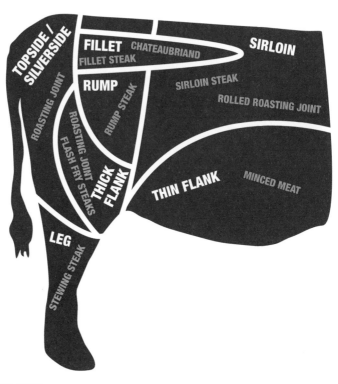

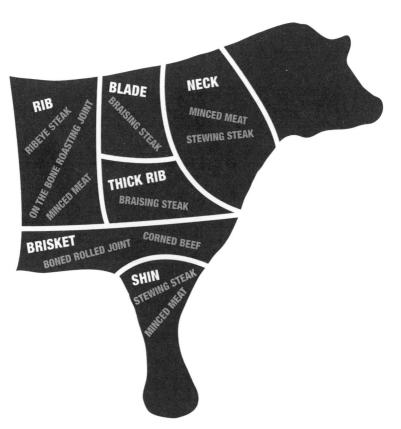

RIB
RIBEYE STEAK
ON THE BONE ROASTING JOINT
MINCED MEAT

BLADE
BRAISING STEAK

NECK
MINCED MEAT
STEWING STEAK

THICK RIB
BRAISING STEAK

BRISKET
BONED ROLLED JOINT   CORNED BEEF

SHIN
STEWING STEAK
MINCED MEAT

ALBANIA
FALEMNDERIT

ANDORRA
GRÀCIES

ARMENIA
MERCI

AUSTRIA
DANKE

AZERBAIJAN
ÇOX SAĞ OL

BELARUS
DZIAKUY

BELGIUM
DANK U

BOSNIA & HERZEGOVINA
HVALA

BULGARIA
BLAGODARYA

CROATIA
HVALA

CYPRUS
EFKHARISTO

CZECH REPUBLIC
DĚKUJI

DENMARK
MANGE TAK

ESTONIA
AITÄH

FINLAND
KIITOS

FRANCE
MERCI

GEORGIA
GMAHD-LOHB

GERMANY
DANKE

GREECE
EFHARISTÓ

HUNGARY
KÖSZÖNÖM

ICELAND
TAKK FYRIR

IRELAND
GO RAIBH MAITH AGAT

ITALY
GRAZIE

KOSOVO
HVALA

LATVIA
PALDIES

LIECHTENSTEIN
DANKE

LITHUANIA
DĖKUI

LUXEMBOURG
MERCI

MACEDONIA
BLAGODARAM

MALTA
GRAZZI

MOLDOVA
MULȚUMESC

MONACO
MERCI

MONTENEGRO
HVALA

THE NETHERLANDS
DANK

NORWAY
TAKK

POLAND
DZIĘKUJĘ

PORTUGAL
OBRIGADO

ROMANIA
MULTUMESC

RUSSIA
SPASIBO

SAN MARINO
GRAZIE

SCOTLAND
TAPADH LEAT

SERBIA
HVALA

SLOVAKIA
D'AKUJEM

SLOVENIA
HVALA

SPAIN
GRACIAS

SWEDEN
TACK

SWITZERLAND
MERCI

TURKEY
SAĞ OL

UKRAINE
DIAKUJU

WALES
DIOLCH

 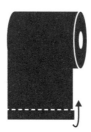 

PULL DOWN ONE AND A HALF SQUARES AND FOLD BACK THE BOTTOM 2 CM

FOLD BACK ANOTHER 2 CM

FOLD UP THE PAPER DEPENDING ON HOW TALL YOU WANT YOUR BASKET

FOLD BACK AN EQUAL AMOUNT OF BOTH EDGES

PULL DOWN PAPER SO HALF THE BASKET IS BELOW ROLL

DONE!

CHEWING GUM
1869
THOMAS ADAMS

AFTER FAILING TO MAKE TOYS USING CHICLE FROM MEXICAN SAPODILLA TREES, ADAMS TRIED CHEWING IT AND LIKED THE TASTE.

CANDY FLOSS
1897
WILLIAM MORRISON AND JOHN C. WHARTON

FIRST SOLD TO THE PUBLIC AT THE WORLD'S FAIR IN 1904. WHARTON WAS A CONFECTIONER; MORRISON WAS A DENTIST.

HOLD A CORK IN EACH HAND AS SHOWN ABOVE

PLACE TIP OF THUMB ON TOP OF CORK IN OPPOSITE HAND

USING INDEX
FINGERS REACH
AROUND, GRAB
CORKS AND
PULL APART

SHOW A FRIEND,
GIVE THEM THE
CORKS, WATCH
THEM FAIL

DOG **HUMAN** **ELEPHANT** **GIRAFFE**

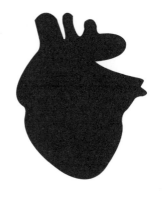

BLUE WHALE

MINI

SPIDER RELEASES NON-STICKY THREAD FROM ITS ABDOMEN INTO THE WIND

SENSING WHEN THE THREAD HAS ATTACHED TO SOMETHING, THE SPIDER MOVES ACROSS IT, RELEASING A LOOSER THREAD

SPIDER CREATES A 'Y' SHAPE WITH MORE NON-STICKY THREAD

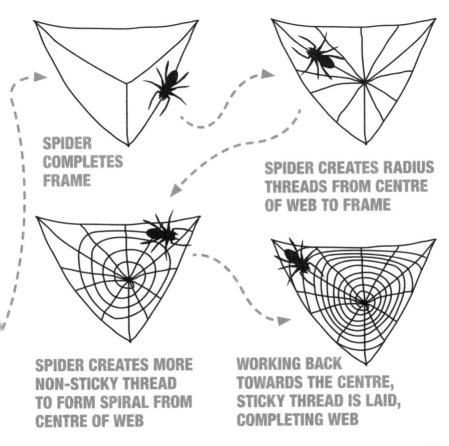

SPIDER
COMPLETES
FRAME

SPIDER CREATES RADIUS
THREADS FROM CENTRE
OF WEB TO FRAME

SPIDER CREATES MORE
NON-STICKY THREAD
TO FORM SPIRAL FROM
CENTRE OF WEB

WORKING BACK
TOWARDS THE CENTRE,
STICKY THREAD IS LAID,
COMPLETING WEB

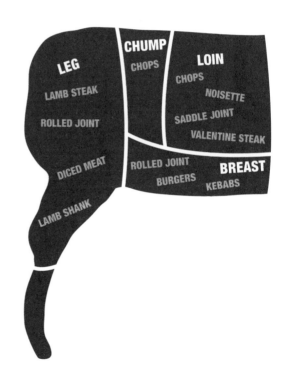

A BLOAT OF HIPPOPOTAMUSES

A HIPPOPOTAMUS

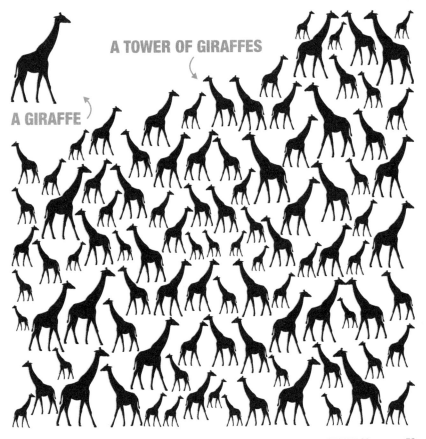

A GIRAFFE

A TOWER OF GIRAFFES

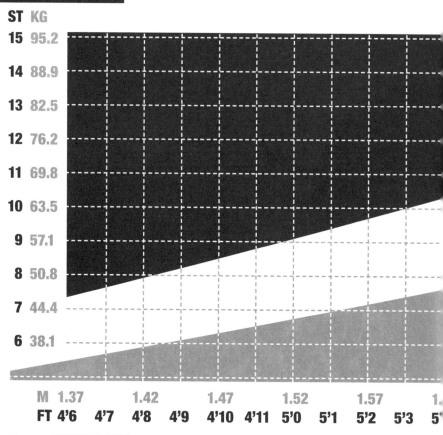

ST KG
15 95.2
14 88.9
13 82.5
12 76.2
11 69.8
10 63.5
9 57.1
8 50.8
7 44.4
6 38.1

M 1.37   1.42   1.47   1.52   1.57   1.
FT 4'6 4'7 4'8 4'9 4'10 4'11 5'0 5'1 5'2 5'3 5'

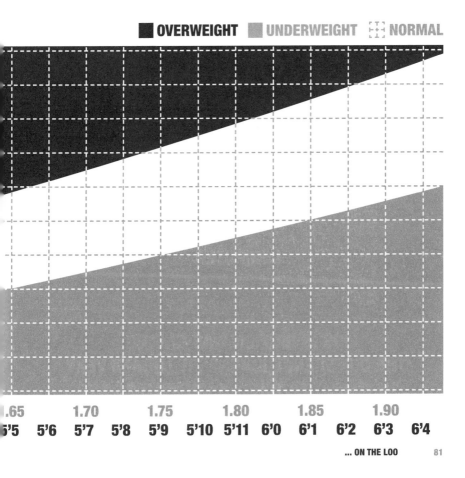

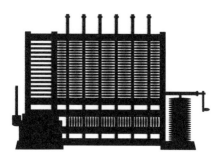

COMPUTER
1822
CHARLES BABBAGE

HIS INVENTION WAS CALLED 'THE DIFFERENCE ENGINE'. IT LOOKED VERY DIFFERENT TO TODAY'S COMPUTERS AND WAS POWERED BY STEAM.

TELEPHONE
1876
ALEXANDER GRAHAM BELL

THE FIRST LONG-DISTANCE TELEPHONE CALL WAS MADE BY BELL FROM BRANTFORD, ONTARIO IN CANADA, TO HIS ASSISTANT LOCATED IN PARIS, ONTARIO, SOME 10 MILES AWAY.

36.8°C

CORE BODY TEMPERATURES OF HUMANS:
<35.0°C HYPOTHERMIA
36.5°C – 37.5°C NORMAL
>37.5°C FEVER
>40.0°C HYPERPYREXIA

**WOOD FROGS IN ALASKA
SURVIVE FOR UP TO
SEVEN MONTHS FROZEN AT
TEMPERATURES OF −18°C.**

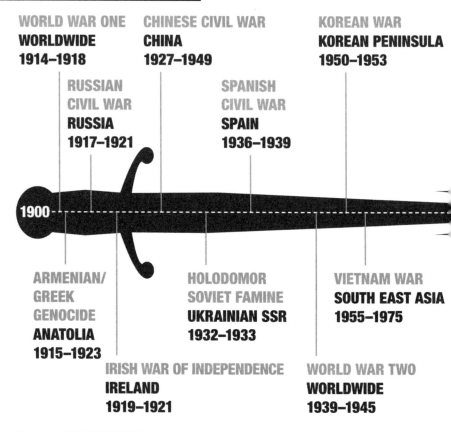

WORLD WAR ONE
WORLDWIDE
1914–1918

CHINESE CIVIL WAR
CHINA
1927–1949

KOREAN WAR
KOREAN PENINSULA
1950–1953

RUSSIAN CIVIL WAR
RUSSIA
1917–1921

SPANISH CIVIL WAR
SPAIN
1936–1939

1900

ARMENIAN/ GREEK GENOCIDE
ANATOLIA
1915–1923

HOLODOMOR SOVIET FAMINE
UKRAINIAN SSR
1932–1933

VIETNAM WAR
SOUTH EAST ASIA
1955–1975

IRISH WAR OF INDEPENDENCE
IRELAND
1919–1921

WORLD WAR TWO
WORLDWIDE
1939–1945

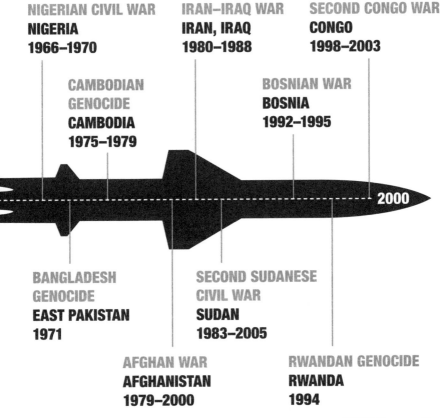

NIGERIAN CIVIL WAR
NIGERIA
1966–1970

IRAN–IRAQ WAR
IRAN, IRAQ
1980–1988

SECOND CONGO WAR
CONGO
1998–2003

CAMBODIAN
GENOCIDE
CAMBODIA
1975–1979

BOSNIAN WAR
BOSNIA
1992–1995

2000

BANGLADESH
GENOCIDE
EAST PAKISTAN
1971

SECOND SUDANESE
CIVIL WAR
SUDAN
1983–2005

AFGHAN WAR
AFGHANISTAN
1979–2000

RWANDAN GENOCIDE
RWANDA
1994

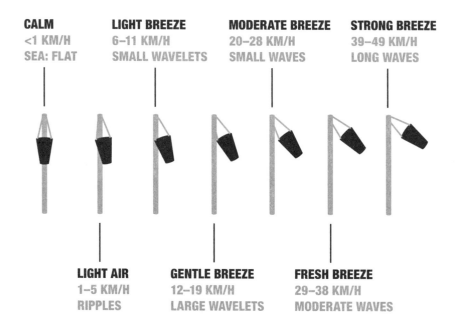

CALM
<1 KM/H
SEA: FLAT

LIGHT BREEZE
6–11 KM/H
SMALL WAVELETS

MODERATE BREEZE
20–28 KM/H
SMALL WAVES

STRONG BREEZE
39–49 KM/H
LONG WAVES

LIGHT AIR
1–5 KM/H
RIPPLES

GENTLE BREEZE
12–19 KM/H
LARGE WAVELETS

FRESH BREEZE
29–38 KM/H
MODERATE WAVES

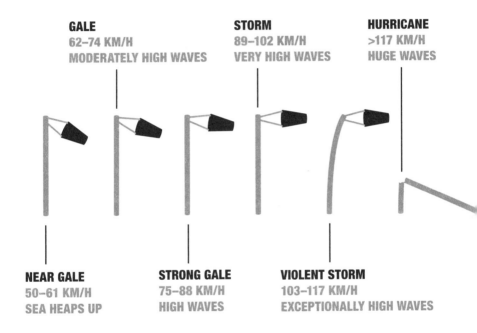

GALE
62–74 KM/H
MODERATELY HIGH WAVES

STORM
89–102 KM/H
VERY HIGH WAVES

HURRICANE
>117 KM/H
HUGE WAVES

NEAR GALE
50–61 KM/H
SEA HEAPS UP

STRONG GALE
75–88 KM/H
HIGH WAVES

VIOLENT STORM
103–117 KM/H
EXCEPTIONALLY HIGH WAVES

ARCTIC OCEAN

GREENLAND SEA

GULF OF BOTHNIA

NORTH SEA

BARENTS SEA

KARA SEA

LAPTEV SEA

EAST SIBERIAN SEA

WHITE SEA

BALTIC SEA

SEA OF OKHOTSK

BLACK SEA

SEA OF JAPAN

BAY OF BISCAY

ARAL SEA

CASPIAN SEA

YELLOW SEA

DEAD SEA

GULF OF OMAN

BAY OF BENGAL

EAST CHINA S

MEDITERRANEAN SEA

SOUTH CHINA SEA

PHILIPPIN SEA

RED SEA

ARABIAN SEA

ARAFURA S

GULF OF GUINEA

GULF OF ADEN

PERSIAN GULF

ANDAMAN SEA

JAVA SEA

INDIAN OCEAN

CELEBES SEA

TIMOR SEA

SOUTH ATLANTIC OCEAN

FLORES SEA

CORAL SEA

SOUTHERN OCEAN

TASMAN SEA

BACK FAT LARD

LOIN

CHOPS
ROASTING JOINTS
SIRLOIN
BACON

LEG

ROASTING JOINTS

GAMMON   HAM

ROASTING JOINTS   BELLY

SPARE RIBS   STREAKY BACON

PANCETTA   SAUSAGES

KNUCKLE

SHANK

HOCK
BRAISING
MEAT

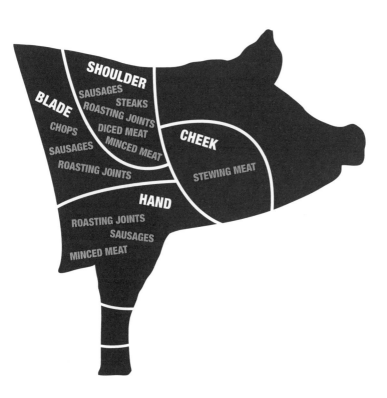

SHOULDER
SAUSAGES
STEAKS
ROASTING JOINTS
DICED MEAT
MINCED MEAT

BLADE
CHOPS
SAUSAGES
ROASTING JOINTS

CHEEK
STEWING MEAT

HAND
ROASTING JOINTS
SAUSAGES
MINCED MEAT

0 MILES

35 MILES

BUDDHISM	CHRISTIANITY	HINDUISM
BUDDHISTS	CHRISTIANS	HINDUS
WHEEL OF DHARMA	CROSS	OM
TRIPITAKA	BIBLE	VEDAS
BUDDHA	JESUS CHRIST	BRAHMA, VISHNU & SHIVA
TEMPLE	CHURCH/CHAPEL	MANDIR

ISLAM

MUSLIMS

CRESCENT AND STAR

THE QURAN

MUHAMMAD

MOSQUE

JUDAISM

JEWS

STAR OF DAVID

TORAH

ABRAHAM

SYNAGOGUE

SIKHISM

SIKHS

KHANDA

GURU GRANTH SAHIB

GURU NANAK

GURDWARA

STICKY TAPE
1922
RICHARD DREW

WHILE TRYING TO SPRAY-PAINT A CAR, DREW CREATED A 2-INCH-WIDE PAPER TAPE WITH A PRESSURE-SENSITIVE ADHESIVE BACKING.

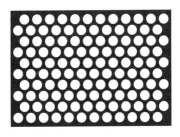

BUBBLE WRAP
1957
ALFRED FIELDING AND MARC CHAVANNES

FIELDING AND CHAVANNES WERE TRYING TO CREATE A 3D PLASTIC WALLPAPER WHEN THEY REALISED WHAT THEY HAD MADE COULD BE USED AS PACKAGING MATERIAL.

EVEREST
ASIA
HIMALAYAS
NEPAL/CHINA
8,850 M

McKINLEY
NORTH AMERICA
ALASKA RANGE
UNITED STATES
6,194 M

SEA LEVEL

ACONCAGUA
SOUTH AMERICA
ANDES
ARGENTINA
6,961 M

KILIMANJARO
AFRICA
TANZANIA
5,885 M

ELBRUS
EUROPE
CAUCASUS
RUSSIA
5,642 M

PUNCAK JAYA
AUSTRALASIA
SUDIRMAN
INDONESIA
4,884 M

MAUNA KEA HAWAII
TALLEST MOUNTAIN
ON EARTH 10,200 M

VINSON
ANTARCTICA
SENTINEL
4,892 M

HIGHEST IS
MEASURED FROM
SEA LEVEL TO SUMMIT.
TALLEST IS MEASURED
FROM BASE TO SUMMIT.
6,000 M ARE UNDER SEA LEVEL.

HONEYBEE SUCKS NECTAR FROM FLOWERS INTO ITS 'HONEY STOMACH'

BEE FLIES BACK TO HIVE; ENZYMES BREAK DOWN COMPLEX SUGARS

HONEYBEE PASSES LIQUID TO HIVE BEE

LIQUID CONTINUES TO BREAK DOWN IN HIVE BEE'S STOMACH

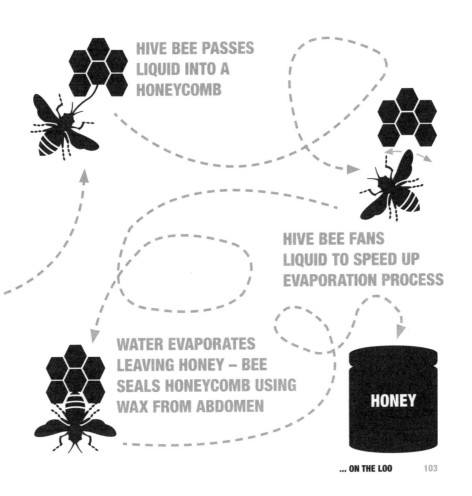

HIVE BEE PASSES LIQUID INTO A HONEYCOMB

HIVE BEE FANS LIQUID TO SPEED UP EVAPORATION PROCESS

WATER EVAPORATES LEAVING HONEY – BEE SEALS HONEYCOMB USING WAX FROM ABDOMEN

HONEY

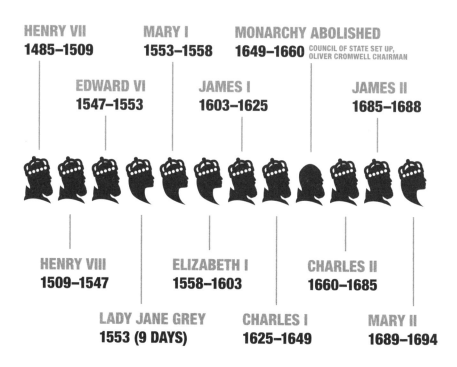

HENRY VII
1485–1509

MARY I
1553–1558

MONARCHY ABOLISHED
1649–1660 COUNCIL OF STATE SET UP,
OLIVER CROMWELL CHAIRMAN

EDWARD VI
1547–1553

JAMES I
1603–1625

JAMES II
1685–1688

HENRY VIII
1509–1547

ELIZABETH I
1558–1603

CHARLES II
1660–1685

LADY JANE GREY
1553 (9 DAYS)

CHARLES I
1625–1649

MARY II
1689–1694

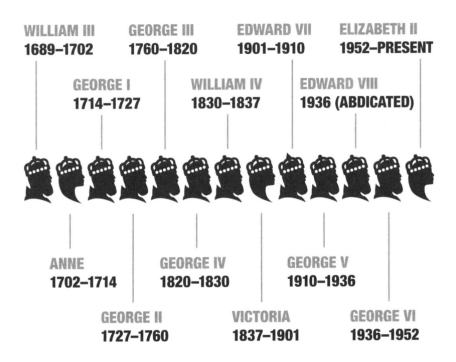

WILLIAM III
1689–1702

GEORGE III
1760–1820

EDWARD VII
1901–1910

ELIZABETH II
1952–PRESENT

GEORGE I
1714–1727

WILLIAM IV
1830–1837

EDWARD VIII
1936 (ABDICATED)

ANNE
1702–1714

GEORGE IV
1820–1830

GEORGE V
1910–1936

GEORGE II
1727–1760

VICTORIA
1837–1901

GEORGE VI
1936–1952

THE HANDLEBAR

THE FU MANCHU

THE ENGLISH

THE HORSESHOE

THE IMPERIAL

THE DALÍ

THE MEXICAN

THE PENCIL

THE TOOTHBRUSH

THE NATURAL

THE WALRUS

THE FAIL

BEAM BRIDGE
E.G. RIO-NITEROI BRIDGE, RIO DE JANEIRO, BRAZIL

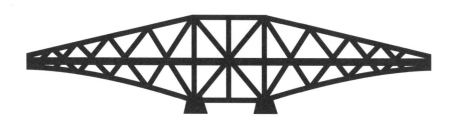

TRUSS BRIDGE
E.G. FORTH BRIDGE, EDINBURGH, SCOTLAND

ARCH BRIDGE
E.G. SYDNEY HARBOUR BRIDGE, SYDNEY, AUSTRALIA

SUSPENSION BRIDGE
E.G. SEVERN BRIDGE, SW ENGLAND TO SE WALES

YO-YO
1000 BC
THE CHINESE

YO-YO-LIKE TOYS ORIGINATED IN CHINA IN THE FORM OF TWO CONNECTED IVORY DISCS WITH A SILK CORD ATTACHED.

FRISBEE
1948
WALTER FREDERICK MORRISON

THE IDEA CAME TO MORRISON WHILE THROWING A CAKE PAN WITH HIS FUTURE WIFE ON THE BEACH IN SANTA MONICA.

A THREE-LEGGED BEAR
A DEAD CROW
A BEE IN A TREE
A TAIL-BITING ALLIGATOR
A PAIR OF KISSING GIRAFFES
A SPIKED CROWN
A SPIDER IN A FIELD OF PINEAPPLES